Copyright © 2024 by Homespun Book Publishing

All rights reserved. This book or any portion thereof may not be reproduced or used in any manner whatsoever without the express written permission of the publisher except for the use of brief quotations in a book review.

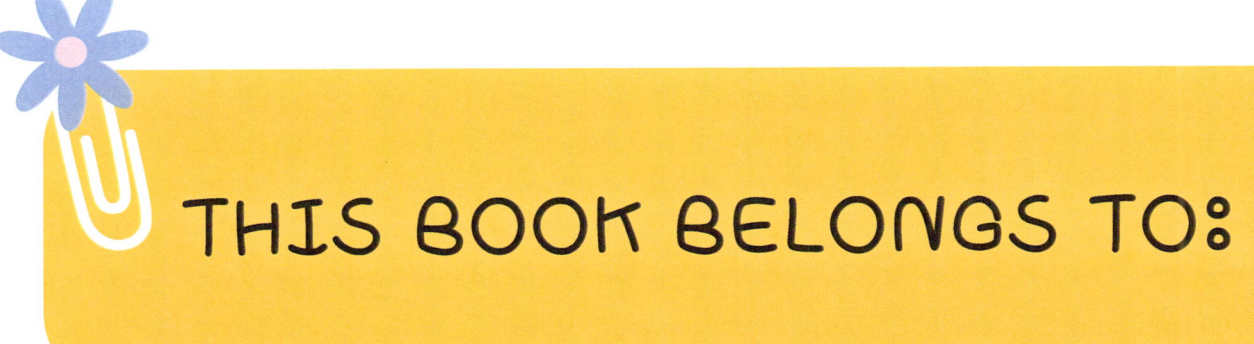

THIS BOOK BELONGS TO:

_____

- -

_____

Your Name

Hi there! I spy you looking at me. Do you spy me?

Who am I? I am the Black-eyed Susan you are seeing.

I have yellow petals on my flowers. Look closely.

You will see red and orange also. My center is black.

That is why I am called Black-eyed Susan.

Hundreds of tiny flowers are in my center. Each holds some nectar. Nectar is what most pollinators want to eat. They sit on me and sip the nectar. While there, they pick up pollen. They move to another bloom. They leave pollen on it. May I tell you more about pollination? Then you can play "I Spy" with flowers and pollinators!

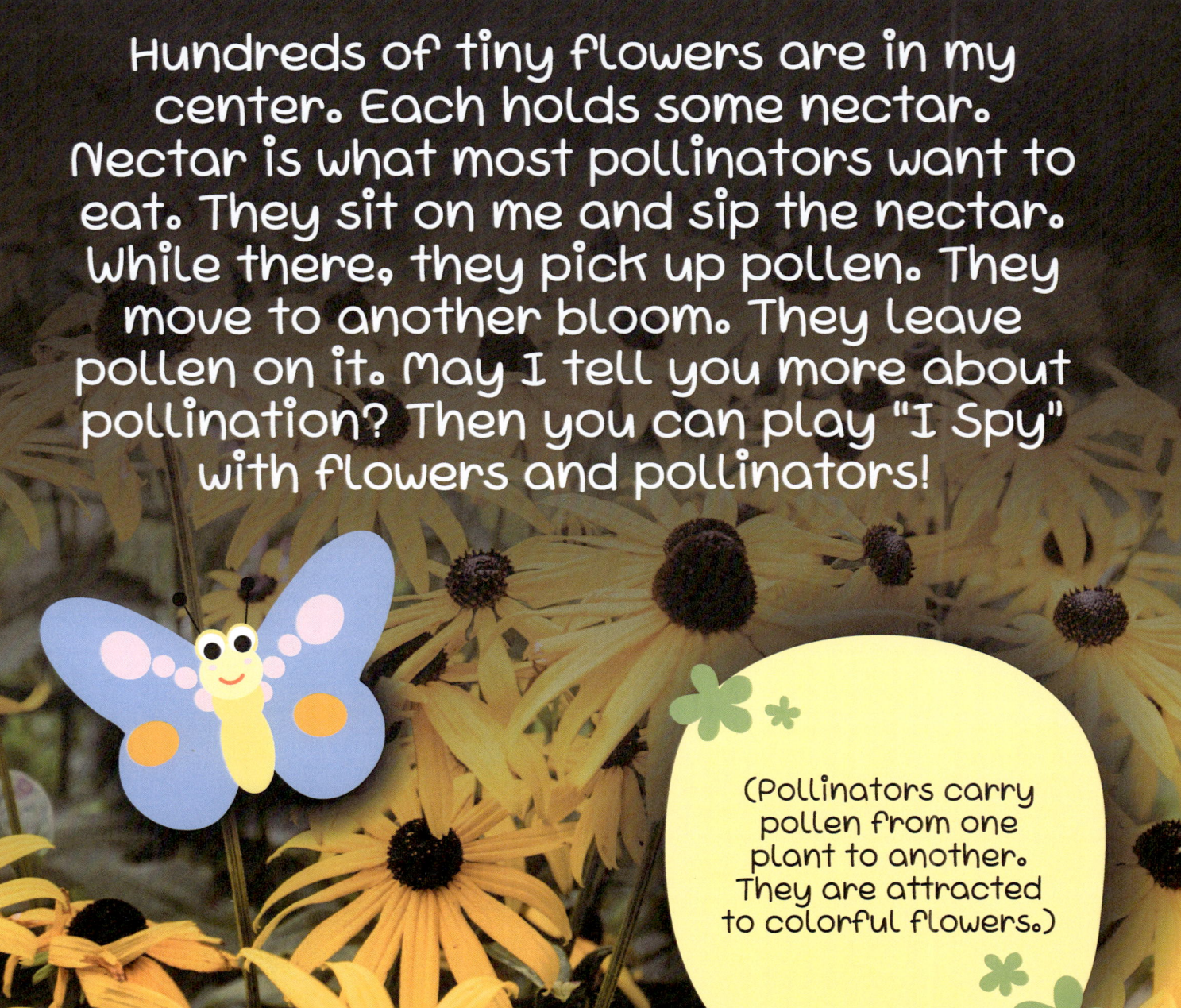

(Pollinators carry pollen from one plant to another. They are attracted to colorful flowers.)

Pollination needs a male flower and a female flower. The female flower has a pistil, where the ovary is located. The ovary is where the seeds develop. The male flower has a stamen. It produces pollen. When the pollinator touches the stamen, the pollen gets on its legs. The pollinator walks or flies to another flower.

When it is on a female flower, it leaves pollen on the pistil. That is called fertilization. The female flower can then produce seeds. Those seeds will become new plants. I can live forever by making seeds. This allows my species to never die.

WHO POLLINATES MY FLOWERS?

Most pollinators are insects. Birds and bats also pollinate some flowers. The wind can pollinate a few plants. As a black-eyed Susan, insects are my friends.

Some of the insects that pollinate flowers are

- bees,
- wasps,
- flies,
- ants,
- moths,
- butterflies,
- beetles,
- and even mosquitoes.

Let's learn about them.

There are hundreds of kinds of bees. Most are native to the United States. Native means we started in this country. Some, like the European Honey Bee, are not native. They are naturalized. That means they started in another country. Now they live in the United States year-round.

Look at a globe. Which continent was the original home of European honey bees?

Native bees come in many sizes. They can be as small as a grain of rice or as large as a quarter, like bumble bees.

Some only visit one kind of flower. Others like many different kinds of flowers.

Why do I like bees? Because I am helping them! They collect pollen to feed their young. They are the only insects that feed my pollen to their young. They even have unique body parts to collect the pollen. They have hairs where the pollen sticks. They have a little basket for pollen on their back legs called the corbicula. They use their mouths to move the pollen to the "crop" inside their body.

A "crop" is like a tiny little stomach. It is used to make honey from pollen.

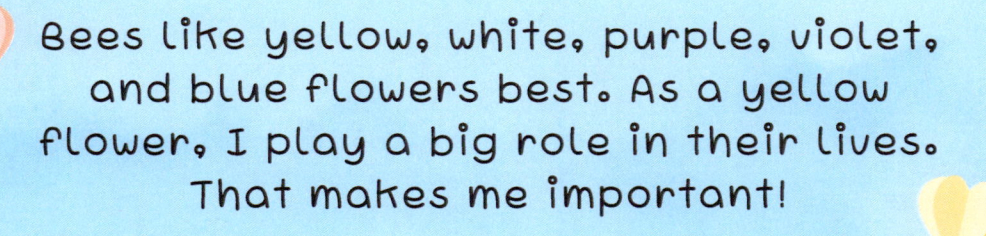

Bees like yellow, white, purple, violet, and blue flowers best. As a yellow flower, I play a big role in their lives. That makes me important!

WASPS

I spy my wasp friend on my sister. My momma told me that people don't like wasps. That is sad to me. I need wasps.

They are good pollinators of flowers. Just as with bees, there are many kinds of wasps. Some are tiny. Some are big. Some sting. Some don't sting.

Wasps visit flowers to eat nectar. They love orchids.

Remember, bees collect pollen and nectar. They feed pollen to their young.

Wasps want my nectar for food. They don't want my pollen. That is because they feed insects to their young, not pollen. It sticks to their feet and legs anyway. They carry it to another flower. They leave pollen on it. Then, I produce seeds.

FLIES

I spy my friend the fly circling my sister. Did you know those pesty flies at picnics can pollinate flowers? They are so important that farmers try to attract them! Farmers even say,

"Thank God for flies!"

Flies like the smell of something rotting. Farmers put raw meat into their mango fields to attract them. Flies eat many things, not just rotting food.

Pollen and nectar are both healthy foods. I think I spy a fly wanting nectar for dessert!

Flies have hairs on their bodies. They fly to a flower. Some of the pollen sticks to the hairs. They move to another flower. They accidentally pollinate the pistil. The flower makes seeds. The seeds become food for many birds and animals. People eat some such as pecans, peas, and sunflower seeds. A few seeds go into the ground. They sprout and become a new plant. The life cycle of plants, animals, and people repeats itself.

This is called a food web.

ANTS

I spy an ant down on the grass. She's my friend too. Ants are pollinators for plants that bloom close to the ground.

The ants crawl on it, looking for food. They may pick up a little pollen. They crawl to another flower and leave it. American ants don't often eat nectar or pollen. They just explore. In a few countries, some ants eat pollen.

Ants can spoil a picnic if they get on your food. The same ants help keep plants reproducing. Plants create oxygen for you to breathe. Ants are your friends, even if they bite or sting you.

MOTHS

I spy something that looks a lot like a butterfly. However, it has a wider body. It is my friend the moth.

Most moths fly and feed at night on night-blooming flowers. Some flowers bloom both day and night. Others bloom one or the other, during the day or during the night. Most moths don't feed on the ones that bloom only during the day.

BUTTERFLIES

Butterflies are beautiful. They look like floating flowers. They go to a flower to eat nectar. Pollen accidentally gets on their legs. It is heavy. They don't like it. They fly to another flower to eat and leave pollen on the new plant. The flower is fertilized. The butterflies feel better because they get rid of the pollen that makes them feel heavy.

Butterflies like red, orange, pink, and purple flowers.

BEETLES

I spy my friend the beetle on the goldenrod clusters of flowers. She is crawling around for nectar but also picking up pollen.

Beetles have a hard covering.

They like white, green, and yellow blooms. They like big flowers and clustering flowers. They need flowers that are open during the day. Magnolia tree blooms are big. Goldenrod has clusters of blooms. Beetles are their friends and pollinate them.

MOSQUITOS

I spy a mosquito crawling up my petals toward my eye.

Did you know that mosquitoes are good pollinators? They are friends of flowers. Like butterflies, they eat nectar.

Boy mosquitoes only eat nectar.

Girl mosquitoes eat it until they lay eggs.

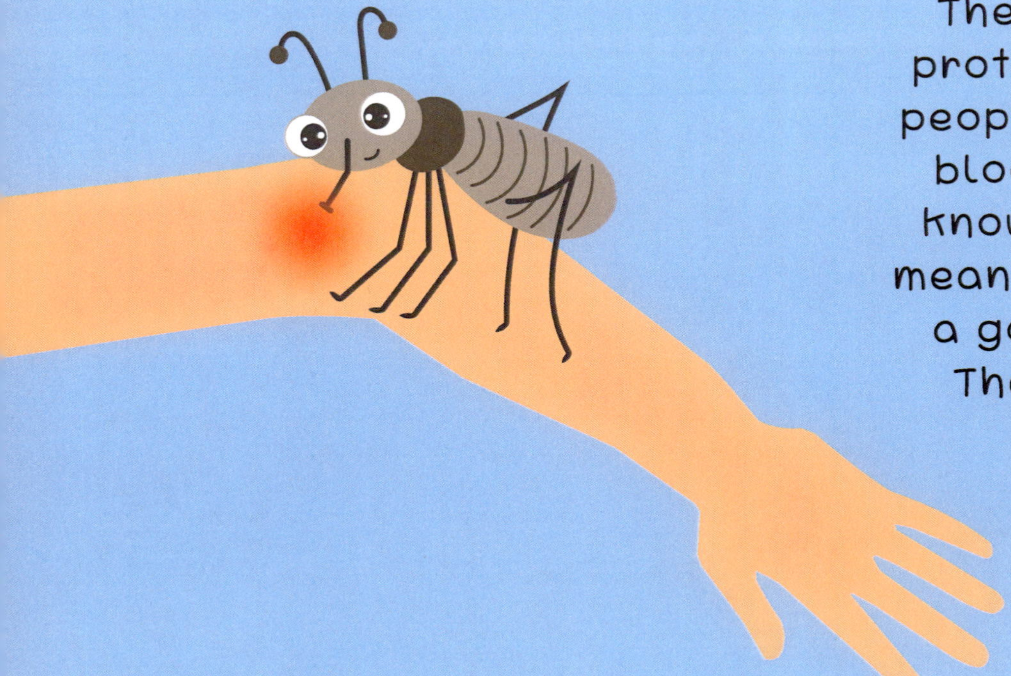

Then, they want protein. They bite people to get some blood protein. I know that sounds mean. They do have a good purpose: They pollinate plants.

 Mosquitoes pollinate some water plants. They pollinate water lilies, water hyacinths, and water lettuce. They also pollinate many types of orchids.

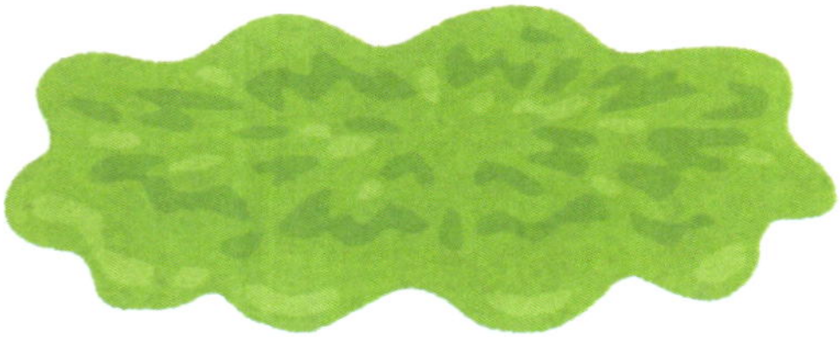

Do I spy a pencil near you? Please tell me three things you learned about pollinators

Would you list them below?

1.

2.

3.

I would also love for you to draw a picture of me!
Do I spy some crayons? Maybe you could color me.

Draw and Color

I am going to say so long for now. I hope you will remember what I have taught you. You can play "I Spy." Why don't you go outside and see if you can spy the pollinators I've told you about?

See if you can locate all the pollinators I have named. I'll be listening to hear you say, "I spy a Black-eyed Susan!" I spy you looking at me now.

Bye from your friend, Black-eyed Susan, who likes to play "I Spy!"

If you have enjoyed reading this book, would you complete an Amazon review? Did you like the book? What was a valuable takeaway? Would you recommend it?

Leave a review!

MEET THE AUTHOR

Linda Smock has been a resident of Pinellas County, Florida since 1969. She grew up in Washington County, Florida, and attended Chipola Junior College and Florida State University. She later attended the University of South Florida. She spent over three decades in public education as a teacher and curriculum supervisor.

She also authored textbooks and worked for 12 years in Christian education. Her hobbies include plants and gardening, watching butterflies and birds, and writing. She is a master gardener with certification from the University of Florida.

She is also the author of Homespun Devotion (Westbow Press), More Homespun Devotion (Amazon), Even More Homespun Devotion (Amazon), Homespun Prayers (Westbow Press), and Homespun Gratitude (Amazon).

Check the Homespun Stories Facebook pages for upcoming events and contests, and watch for the next book.

Thank You

Linda Smock

Also Available on Amazon!

Purchase
"Just Call Me Honey"
TODAY!

Scan Here

www.ingramcontent.com/pod-product-compliance
Lightning Source LLC
Chambersburg PA
CBRC101144030426
42337CB00008B/65